Unapologetically Feminist

All rights reserved. No part of this publication may be reproduced, distributed, or transmitted in any form by any means, including photocopying, recording, or other electronic methods without the prior written permission of the author, except in the case of brief quotations embodied in reviews and certain other noncommercial uses permitted by copyright law. For permission requests, write to the author at the address below.

Copyright © 2022 Urvashi Bundel
unapologeticallyfem@gmail.com
www.urvashibundel.com

ISBN 978-0-578-38216-6

Edited and designed by Tell Tell Poetry
Illustrations by Rulos de Carbón and Tell Tell Poetry

Printed in the United States of America

First Printing, 2022

For Anna

Contents

World on Fire

Torchbearer of Apocalypse	5
Baobab: Falling of the Giants	7
You Sit in Potočari!	8
Dandelion Seeds	10
Fiction in Us	12
Under the Abyssinian Sky	13
Patterns	15
Afghanistan: A Twenty-Year-Long Jest	17
All in the Name of Death	18
Irrigation of Patriotism	20
Colorism	22
Between the Ashes	24
Great Expectations	26
A Reply: Women, Law, and Cairo	27
Elevation. Education.	31
Margin of Error	32
Cleopatra Must've Felt Lonely	35
On Turtles and Women	37
Child Brides	38
A Mutilated Mutiny	39

How My Week Ended on a Tuesday!	41
My Confidence in Humanity	42
Stupefied Shores	43
Kilifi, the Goat	45
We Fly	47
Delhi: A Damsel in Distress	48
2020: The Year I Dived	50
Bystander	51
Taking Chances	52
Thoughts in Quarantine	53
In Providential Times of Mankind	54
The Conversationalist	55
To Delusional Instapoets	57
Digital Slavery	59
Faithful	61
Mes Amis Félins	62
"Hamsteren" Is to Hoard	64
Death of a Spider in Times of Social Distancing	66
Not in the Audience	68

Watch Me Burn

A Girl Who Reads	73
Making of a Unicorn	76
Woman of Color	78
Containment	79

Watch Me Burn	80
Born a Debt	82
Floating on the Wings of Faith	84
A Miniscule Familiarity with Danger	85
Feast on Me, Afrika!	89
The Corporate Jungle: A Memoir to Skyscrapers in Tokyo	92
Reading in Rage, Writing in Tranquility	95
Secret Admirers of Feminism	96
Women and Confidence	98
Resilience	100
In the Best of Fall, I Rise	101
Discourses with Fear	102
Phantasmagoria	104
Sedation of a Vision	111
Café of Humbleness	112
Ancestral Tribute	114
Chastity Test	116
Mimosa Stories Retold	117
Synonyms for Happiness	119
Learn to Pick Your Price	121
Perspectives	122
Kotoba	124
Mental Health	125
Finding a Muse	126

No Wonder Rumi Fell in Love So Easily!	127
La Couleur Du Sang	128
A Library Kind of Love	130
Zanzibari Rhapsody: A Feline Encounter	132
An Affair with Thoughts	134
Moringa Enlightenments	135
Stop and Smell the Roses!	137
My Polish Grill	138
Characterization of a Unicorn	139
A Tiger's Shadow	141

From the Ashes

Mermaid Dreams for a Decade	145
Rise of a New Decade	146
A Bullish Feminism	147
Womanned Up!	151
Solitary Hope	153
Blessings of the Eighth of March	154
Pashmina Thoughts	155
Howling: Times of Isolation	156
Science of Humanities	157
Legacy	158
Make It Count	159
At Church, Every Single Day!	160
Circumcised Halos	161

A Cinderella Hour	162
When Dreaming Is an Urgency	164
A Soliloquy for Libra Season	166
Jerusalem	167
Weaving a Republic!	168
In Memory of Memorial Day	169
Waiting for the Sun to Rise	172
Duotones and Undertones	173
On Good and Bad Days	174
Elderflower Women	175
Karnak Café: A Tribute	177
Wild Openings!	180
July's Buck Moon	182
A Better Day	184
A Woman's Prerogative	185
Sparrow	186
On Never Giving Up!	187
The Art of Climbing	188
About the Author	191

Acknowledgments

Much of this manuscript was written during my daily commute between home and work in Tokyo, Cairo, Washington DC, New York, and Addis Ababa. Because of this, I would like to acknowledge in particular the Tokyo Metro authorities, the New York Greyhound Lines bus service, and Uber drivers for making the task of writing on public transport so delightful.

I thank Starbucks in Japan and India for tolerating me on most weekends. I thank the cyber fraudsters for making my account nice and clean, which allowed me more time and focus towards this collection.

Finally, I would like to thank Mr. Mohamed Abla, a renowned Egyptian artist, for offering three of his feminist paintings as inspiration.

Unapologetically Feminist

World on Fire

Torchbearer of Apocalypse

How strange it will be, one day,

To solemnly let go of all the miseries—

Decadent halls of fame and their ferocious chandeliers

Piercing into our eyes, the glass

Embedded in the existence of human suffering.

Not until the days of the hermit did we realize

How futile were the sinister and their schemes

To forsake our youth into chiseled wars

That we never asked for.

The fumes that rose through cartons

Burned in despair.

We couldn't even tell the color of their blood,

Yet we divided them into flags and heritage,

Into opportunistic moments,

Longing

To isolate into the woods of affirmations

That our mothers used to sing.

It is not the darkness that is evil.
It is the lack of torchbearer
That makes it unbearable!

Baobab: Falling of the Giants

The stature of their significance,

Like elders of a community,

Standing wide and tall

With roots receding into the heavens,

As if telling us all to stand still

In accord and silence.

Only to observe the power of rising,

For there are greater truths in life

Than the mere cacophony of ugly chitchats.

Only to observe the fate of falling

Into an abysmal trench of our own doings!

You Sit in Potočari!

You sit curled yet unbridled,

Like a Bosnian doll made of bone china.

You sit like a volcano

Digressing

Its every flow.

You sit like a thought, so shattering.

You sit like reparations unpaid.

You sit like a tethered history of ignominy,

Dreaming of catching that last overcrowded bus.

You sit like an unforgotten guilt

In the vulnerable hearts of these widows,

In the demolished souls of Dutch soldiers,

In the tyrant hearts of this world.

You sit like a discourse unfinished.

You sit like alpine asters,

Spreading on your body like moss.

And yet you sit like an angel

Peacefully buried

Under the dark clouds of Potočari.

You sit in Srebrenica!

Dandelion Seeds

Floating like the unwanted furs of Eskimos

In hot Indian summers of the sultanate,

The unbridled touch of their bristles

On the skin,

Chastening as

The dried-out tears

And demonizing fears

Of a religious gathering

Catering to the yellows and the greens,

The oranges and pinks,

The purples and the white.

Like the dandelion seeds

All mushed up in a haze

With no room to breathe

Or reminisce about their frolic past.

Every molecule interlocked as if

Stuck to the idolized identities of the present

On the skin

Of fear-mongering men

Like the dandelion seeds,

Chastening as if

Perturbed by the class

And its classy men!

Fiction in Us

The universe wrote a fiction in us.

It's called fear.

Yet we tear every page,

Dry the ink and quill,

Wrench our imagination,

Rewriting

To turn it into nonfiction.

What a fictitious living

Of a brave soul,

Of a body that grows roots

Deep underground

In stupendous illusion!

Under the Abyssinian Sky

Written under lockdown in a forest at the border between Ethiopia and Sudan.

Unsure what hisses so loud

In the surrounding bushes

Each night, next to this door

In this compound.

It swallows my fears

Into a greater fear,

Not sure what exactly I must escape.

Is it the humans, animals, or gods?

Humans are desolate of soul.

Animals are craving of imagination.

Gods are desolate of trust.

Land mines are soothing orphans.

But worst of all are Freudian assumptions,

Relegated to demystifying the human psyche

In the construal of incidents.

You wish you knew better now

Than you experienced then.

Abyssinia is where this state lies

In my mind,

In your psyche!

Patterns

Cajoled by the impetus of dreams,

I often daydream.

What should we surrender to?

God or his preachers,

Learning or its teachers,

Land or its fights,

Left or its rights?

A subdued debate.

I often claim to understand

And often fail to acknowledge

Patterns!

A claim so strong

That often torments

Oceans and wrecks ships.

Patterns

Of humans and their earthly desires.

Patterns

Of ambitions and its quagmires.

Patterns

Of ancestors and descent.

Patterns

Of ownership and rent!

Afghanistan:
A Twenty-Year-Long Jest

We pass down the streets of restitution

To discover fragments of desolate attitude,

Of broken dreams and symphonies,

Only to find more despair and longing

Careening its claws into our bones,

Burying its fangs into our skin.

All dusted into trite jokes,

Renewed grief, and solitude.

All in the Name of Death

All in the name of death,

They circled and crisscrossed a divided hall

Like a chess board

Laden with its kings and queens.

All in the name of death,

They bartered exotic goods and married widows.

They sailed into violent harbors,

Trading fish and desolate dreams.

They captured young damsels of the polite type

And chained innocent animals of the wild type.

They enchanted snake charmers and their mysterious pipes,

All in the name of death,

Claiming:

Fortunate are those who are both charmed

And afraid of death,

Not because it's surreal

Or offers a promise to deliver you to the overflowing Grail,

But because you know

You must immediately end what you started—

That conquest,

That war,

That love—

And banish all inhibitions

That started years ago,

Before you call it

A legacy.

But because you know,

Once you say, *You're beautiful*,

She will nod and say,

So be it.

All in the name of death!

Irrigation of Patriotism

As you see past the cavalries

And hoist the flag

Of glory and sacrifice,

Dive a little deeper into your conscience.

Not to seek solace from the noise

Inside,

But to disengage from discussions

Outside.

In theories of the intangible past,

In thinking patterns of amateurs,

In the levity of ideas,

In the extremism of words,

Patriotism

Is not nationalism.

Let that sink in.

Distill the meaning crystal clear,

Anointed with facts,

Before pouring it down

Down the naïve throats

Of your brothers.

You see: muddy waters

Never irritated mindfulness,

Especially

In places it does not exist,

In lands where it was never known,

And above all,

Inside you.

So if you must engage,

Engage with yourself.

Weigh up

The sacrifices you made,

The fields you irrigated,

Before you stand

In front of the flag

That did all that for you!

Colorism

I am an artist.

Ever since kindergarten, I was taught

White is a color.

To my surprise, when I came to America,

I was identified as "colored."

America helped me assimilate this change

From "colour" to "color."

What it couldn't persuade me of, though, was that

White is not a color.

After all, to my naked eyes, they all reacted to water

And dissolved the same way.

Suddenly, I saw my years of education begin to dissolve

In front of my eyes.

Suddenly, I wasn't sure

If I was failing my teachers or if my teachers had failed me.

Suddenly, I wasn't sure

If it was me or everyone else who had turned color-blind.

Unapologetically,

I couldn't paint that logic then.

I cannot paint that logic now.

To me, red was the color of blood then.

Red is the color of blood now!

Between the Ashes

The soul is such a host,

It uncouthly dips its toes

Into every mirage it encounters.

Such is the irony of my feet!

Into waters so uncertain,

So deep and banks so narrow,

I find myself drowning

In the hands of the clock each time!

And whenever I do, I sink—

Sunk into the whirlpools of time and nature,

On the rocky shores of time

And of nature so undiscovered!

Such an interesting encounter,

I hardly relate each time it arises—

A rise so fated yet untouched,

A rise so desired yet unbridled!

Grains of sand seem more fortuitous now,

For they know where they belong.

They know why they were thrust

In and out of the flamboyant desert storm!

For they know the true nature—

The nature of rise and fall.

But I, a ship so beguiled,

Never learned about the true nature,

Neither from the sands nor from the seas!

Mirages abound and I still float,

For what use is a diamond

If it cannot cut its own blood

And cease bleeding vulnerability!

Time, you bake bread in a kiln,

Bricks in a furnace,

And then cremate in chambers.

Either your fire's too holy or mine too unsophisticated

To see no difference

Between the ashes you create!

Great Expectations

It's good to be a woman

In some countries.

Unlike your male counterparts,

No one expects you

To work overtime,

To live alone,

To earn more.

No one taunts you

To study harder.

Basically,

No one blames you

When you fail

Because

That is what is

Expected of you!

A Reply: Women, Law, and Cairo

The poem is a response to the ideology presented by an Egyptian minister. The Independent, November 2017.

It's hard to say every woman faces that.

After all, it's not just a misogynist world.

It's also black and white.

Though mine is pretty colored.

I see that every morning

In the mirror.

So I pull a Gaston act

Only to carry on!

In the aftermath of an extravagant soirée,

Sealed with texts too risqué,

A bad aftertaste!

Feeling ambushed

Into one-line minimalisms,

Paragraphs are meant for circles

That lack corners for small talk.

So recalibrate your preferences

Or else let your Mario hit a wall!

Not on the sidewalks though,

Where passersby will pilfer your yin and yang

And cab drivers honk the life

Out of your soul.

On an empty street—

Too empty,

Not for the faint-hearted.

Distilling lascivious brews of remarks

Each morning

Is an intoxicating process!

Even the Nile seems to sway with it.

Weeds of guilt and dismay get dumped

When predators race around it,

But that's just how mornings look!

Evenings are a different story.
Reaching the same sidewalk
Is a revolution in itself,
But you still put on a wishful thought,
Hoping for change!
Shrills of unicorn-busters come racing
In pairs
Of piercing stares and screams.
Did my anatomy call for an auction?
Perplexed, I see my reflection
In the windowpane:
Hair's in an updo and all's veiled!
What's wrong? I wonder.
Veils really don't matter sometimes.
So much happens in and around them.

Diplomacy is an unnatural art
I seldom paint.

Even less on days I emancipate Bloody Mary,

Days I prescribe to only one filter.

No, not above my shoulders.

It preserves constitutional well-being and pseudo-egos.

The world isn't looking for one more martyr, you see.

One stain is enough

Because one size fits all: Woman!

1. Gaston refers to the self-indulgent, fictional character of the famous traditional fairy tale, "Beauty and the Beast," written by Gabrielle-Suzanne Barbot de Villeneuve in 1740.

2. Mario refers to the fictional protagonist of the *Mario* video game franchise, owned by Nintendo and created by Japanese video game designer Shigeru Miyamoto.

Elevation. Education.

In the beginning, me educating you

About the existence of racism and misogyny,

And pretending not to understand

Maps would be kind of cute.

But gradually, this would stop working

Because my patience would run out

And your education would backfire,

Each of us ending up learning about

The goodness of the education of men and women!

Margin of Error

When you do not comprehend

How someone could be virtuous

But without voting rights.

When you do not understand

How someone could be overqualified

But without a job.

When you do not understand

How someone could be talented

But without a nationality.

When you do not understand

How someone fled his or her country barefoot

But without an identity card.

When you do not comprehend

How someone works three jobs

But still cannot meet their rent.

When you do not understand

Why your government welcomes aliens

Who might uplift your economy

But who can't speak your tongue.

When you do not understand

Why someone's riches do not equate to their morals.

When you do not understand

How the color of your skin affects your job prospects.

When you do not understand

Why someone sits with her family

At a heavily patrolled border,

Detained

Under dark grey clouds of rain,

Which pours down on her half-buried feet,

Being stateless.

When you do not understand the socio-economic layers

Of gender disparity.

When you do not comprehend

How someone could be born in the backyard of bombshells

But still aspire to be a doctor.

When you do not comprehend

That race has nothing to do with competence,

You are truly privileged!

Cleopatra Must've Felt Lonely

At the intoxicating corniche,

As blue waves hit rocks

Of Mediterranean salt,

Distant from the one on the savanna

Where prides of lions preen

But here,

Even cats seem to scurry under chairs

Like hopeless minions,

Feeding themselves on beggary

And unresolved guilts.

They pounce on every opportunity.

Every lick is distasteful,

Piercingly unsettling.

Why do I need an escort?

Why do I need an escort on a wheelchair?

Why do I need paparazzi?

Why do I need paparazzi with no cameras?

So mouthy,

Generously bequeathing

Undesired attention,

Despicable claims,

Bewitching marathons,

Floundering alleys.

Ancient Alexandria wasn't like this.

Mark Antony must've had it easy

And Cleopatra

Must've felt lonely!

On Turtles and Women

Turtles and women both age slowly.

Both live long and sometimes,

Just sometimes, become lucky charms.

From crippled feet in tiny shoes,

Ringed into being "comfort women."

From a fairy tale of walking down the aisle

In a cascade of fedoras waving in appreciation.

From damsels in distress in pornographic fantasies,

Reclaiming their freedom in chains.

From the veiled beauties of Tashkent,

Singing the glories of its lost mountains and men.

From dissolute streets with hidden Klimt treasures.

Just like the turtles,

The voices of women age slow

And die hard!

Child Brides

Education is a city

Filled with streetlights and philanthropists,

Filled with beggars, saints, artists, and preachers,

Filled with wine glasses that clink

And with banality and its stink,

Filled with pastures lush and green,

Filled with debauchery and kink,

Filled with necessary hardships

Like thunderbolts and rifts.

Education is a casino

Filled with erudite, classy men.

It is a city of war.

But

A good education is a nation.

It is the world.

So why forcibly marry a child

Instead of educating one?

A Mutilated Mutiny

It is tough to think in her shoes—

Also because she's got none.

A boisterous lot of hounds came last night

Under the willow tree.

On rocks, the bloodstains still remain

From her brother's skull,

The tattered skirt she wears,

And the hyenas that lurk around

With genitally mutilated men in armor.

What's more dangerous? she wonders.

Haunted by the ghosts of the remains

And shoddy shrubs in the backyard,

She recedes into the jungles.

The girl must eat

And the hyenas too.

In a fight to gather firewood,

She returns burned again from the bushes,

This time with the title of *witch*.

A shovel and a concern,

Both looming low.

What could've gone wrong?

With her body

That made the world so crimson,

What could she do to live better?

Or maybe she could just inhale

Less dusty air.

She digs out a dagger

Entrenched in the sore-holes of her ancestral home

And mutilates herself.

And now she is one of them too!

How My Week Ended on a Tuesday!

It's just that there's so much sin

Laden deftly in every crevice of this week

That my week seems to be over already.

Over—on a Tuesday!

As I recorded how a brother raped his sister—

Line by line, linen by linen—

The goblet of blood brimmed with fire,

Overflowing

The nerves, so stained.

I watched her dignity burn into a pit so dark,

Banished from the high walls of Khartoum.

I choked hard, very hard,

On the fumes of brackish humanity

As her tears profusely rolled down her cheeks,

Pleading with me not to tell her nieces

Why she never found a man,

For her prize was to be disowned.

Also to be circumcised.

My Confidence in Humanity

My confidence keeps breaking

In you, in me,

So unabashedly

That now, each time it crashes,

It turns on a dime,

Smirking and saying,

Aww, again? Who cares!

And right there, it dusts off

Some more from the shelf.

Stupefied Shores

Where intestines choke on opium

Receding into the bloodstream like diffused fairy tales,

Destined for doom and incompetence.

Where daedal hands of nature allure wilderness,

Promiscuity, and lust,

Pouring their egos and indignities into one.

Where booking-dot-com ratings are the king,

Crowning endless summers of scorching shores,

Undefined bikini lines,

And seventy-five-year-old Maasai love stories,

Walking the hall of fame in its utmost glory,

Bedecked with sullied rumors and dashing *daladala*,

Both chasing our souls.

Where, from blinding lights and social status,

Men rule the roost.

Where days pass by like dark clouds of dismalness,

Vying for silver coins and dreaming of tanzanite.

Where life seems to crawl in insobriety,

As if coyly renting its steps from the walking dead.

Or shall I say, smoking ghosts?

Where lungs are pitted with black smog,

Curtailing our linguistics and breath.

Mostly both at the same time,

Not knowing which came first.

Only to utter in profound deference:

Karibu, Zanzibar!

Kilifi, the Goat

What kind of place is Kilifi?

A cave with invisible radars

Patronizing sea animals.

A desert with no shiny pebbles,

Stealing sunshine from their porous divides

Like puritans of pearls, oysters

Opening and closing,

Only to survive one extra day.

What kind of place is Kilifi?

Where days end before they begin,

Where wine flows down the chimney racks,

As if all was said in smoke

Without pursuit of divinity or love.

What kind of place is Kilifi?

An island full of lamenting fishermen

Or a place where no crows peck their nests.

What kind of place is Kilifi?

Which isolates heavens, craving vision,

And baobab bark is dying of thirst.

What kind of place is Kilifi?

Do angels sing in vain there?

Or do hermits reside for free?

What kind of place is Kilifi?

Where no desires meet.

Or is it a goat,

Hanging on a Moroccan dream,

Desiring to be claimed

And seen?

We Fly

*In the aftermath of the mass cremation of
COVID-19 victims in New Delhi in April 2021.*

So we fly on the wings of faith,

In the name of faith, passion, or creed,

Roads all converging on a distant fate.

We surreptitiously flap our wings

In desperation,

In hope,

In anger,

In dismay—

All gasping for oxygen,

All foraging for a cylinder!

Delhi: A Damsel in Distress

O what a sweet retreat you are

To my skin and my jaws,

To everyone's crow's-feet!

Churning the history of dolled-up

Kings and queens,

Seeking a mirage of religion and atrocities

Amalgamated with disparaged icons

And their unflattering deeds.

The beatitude of Lodi Gardens

In shards of turquoise, pink, and violet,

In the form of a rare X-ray scan,

As if that's all that's left of them.

O what a sweet retreat you are

To the everlasting pain

In my lungs!

Like dissolute air

In an exercise to conjure.

Unlike the Mughals,

My dilemma perspires—

For the more I breathe,

The less air my lungs get!

2020: The Year I Dived

Standing still like hermits in the sea of time,

Sure that there's much more to life

Than being a meaningless bunch.

There's joy in being stoic,

Something that we quintessentially adjourned this year.

Lo! The year ends—

Casting its crimson light on our fears,

Excavating centuries of biases against color,

Ripping cold veins of collectivism

And the pretense it demands,

Rampaging through Wall Street

And its bewitching wildfires,

Shattering majestic powerhouses into little blue hearts,

All starving for health insurance and food stamps.

Bystander

Be passive.

Live passive.

I promise

No harm shall befall you.

It's the safest spot on Earth,

Albeit a bit crowded—

The spot of a bystander!

Taking Chances

It would've been good.

It could've been wonderful.

It would've been nice.

It could've been superbly wise.

Why?

Is all I am asking.

Harrowing worries

Are often about the past or future,

But regrets are made of the present—

Of could-haves

And would-haves.

So instead of sorrows and sighs,

I choose to ask:

Why?

Thoughts in Quarantine

Life's a joke.

No one ever told me.

If only I had known that earlier,

I'd be the envy of the clowns,

Aspiration of the weary kings,

Wrath of the forsaken,

Messiah to the religious linchpins!

In Providential Times of Mankind

Isn't it a privilege?

To be a beacon of adventure to someone's life?

How fortuitous of you to lead that life,

When your less-than-twenty-percent of a crusade

Makes up for someone's one-hundred-percent of sanity!

The Conversationalist

Between entrenchments of death and sophistication,

Between tongue-twister and cavalry,

There was a conversationalist,

Adept in weaving the most blinding dreams

Like a gazelle galloping across the African terrains,

Day and night.

The power of his utter monotonous gaffes

Raised eyebrows across the hallways of Midtown,

Amongst its luminous men and women.

So unwontedly

Wanting to alight the world on a matchstick,

He craved to burn

Both ends

Of power and its treacherous majesty.

He worried more often than not

About how good he was

To bind them all with his tongue,

Rupture them like fireflies of night.

About how good he was to not run callously into lives.

About how good he was to pave ways

For those undecided on God

And those still meekly pondering a way to Him.

Wishing, one day,

He shall be granted silence from the village,

He held onto the old patterns of beliefs,

Swept anything and everything

Right under the carpet,

Wishing no one that would see.

But every time the rug spoke,

He'd famously respond by saying:

I am not a conversationalist.

You are.

But you don't even know.

To Delusional Instapoets

Not to underplay,

But either you're so flooded

With creative juices

That you can release one "inspirational quote"

Each day

Or you don't care whether it is

Inspirational at all.

For what kind of creativity

Is that?

That flows without acknowledgment

Of its own environment,

Of its own pitfalls,

Of its own biorhythms.

For what kind of creativity

Is that?

That doesn't know how to

Pause,

That floats on cloud nine

Each day, such that

It overlooks its own sexuality

And staggers,

While still claiming

To be sober!

Digital Slavery

It must be monotonous

To persistently gaze at an infinite void

Between white spaces,

Disillusioned by the information it dispels,

Misled by the catastrophes it embarks on

Through the human soul and mind.

So I gaze at you, unexpectedly, with empathy and pain.

Why have you been unable to declutter

Your consciousness from this space?

Why do you enslave yourself every passing hour?

Why do you sow these seeds of poison ivy each day?

Why do you isolate yourself

From your spiritual destiny each night?

I see you climb down

These euphoric cyber pipelines like a burglar,

Clasping tightly onto the tall, futile walls

Of a binary dungeon,

Unable to sanitize the mental space.

I ask myself: *When will you ever learn how to differentiate?*

When will you learn how to prioritize?

So I watch you from the sidelines of this digital divide.

My roots grow thicker and wide,

Entrenched deeply into human suffering,

Incapable of holding mindful conversations

Or thought or human sentiments.

So I watch you from the sidelines of this digital divide—

How your life is invaded

By the sagacious algorithmic invaders,

How you have no control over it.

So I grin in apathy and disconcerted agony,

Painstakingly cataloging answers

To questions you never asked!

Faithful

They swung between the chains of monogamy
Like pendulums
Insidiously falling from Galileo's hand.
The thought ruffled their feathers—
Shackles, at least that's what people told them.
They waltzed and laughed
Through merry escapades,
Through all-night erotic cabarets
Like mammoths and beasts chasing tinkerbells,
Like fireflies flaming nightstand lamps,
Deserting sweet-scented pianos
At the keynotes of Venetian masquerades.
But when they returned to their hollow domiciles,
They wished they had someone—
Someone who loved them too,
But loved them only.
Yet their barmy heads and egoistic jabs
Often led them to wonder:
What's monogamy then?

Mes Amis Félins

On every street, these vagabonds, despicable cats,

Are stashed in dark corners of detritus,

Bequeathing their appetite for beggary.

Lo! In the land of pharaohs, the opposite happens—

Amassing enough praises and cuddles for their age,

Whether it is their first or ninth life. Here each is prized,

Like capital in a world of wage.

Neither rest by sundown, nor any relief at dawn,

Just a walk down a dimly lit road of Gezira.

I hallucinate at every screech,

At every piece of dirt in the road,

At every torn piece of cloth dangling from the trees,

While they lounge in their regal dwellings,

Hastily made of dregs in domiciles of drains.

I wonder, should they express dissent about living this way,

A mere strike against the stale bread and milk,

The world would witness another uprising at Tahrir Square.

Bastet reigns in each of them still, though silently,

But profusely still earns reverence here.

Unlike in India, where they endure the boot-lash,

Of every passerby, the detestations of every woman—

Piteous in starvation, condemned to perish.

But here, hardly oppressed, they raise their heads

And humankind rues at their every cry.

Buried with kings and legends of mummies,

Kitties still rule this part of the world, unlike the curs,

Chewing upon the very bones of their masters.

If ever they were alerted to the deprivation,

If ever they were kidnapped for their condescension,

May someone disembark, mes amis félins!

May someone tug the insentient tails!

"Hamsteren" Is to Hoard

Hamsteren is a Dutch word that means hoarding and relates to a behavior where people or animals accumulate food or other items. This title came about at a time when there were news flashes about how people had begun to hoard groceries the moment countries began their COVID-related lockdowns.

Our tears have begun to germinate seeds,

Frigidly buried

In the abandoned ruin of this lighthouse,

Clenched fists and pulsating hearts

Vowing to never let go, as if

Their jaws, full of vigor and dreams,

Were prepared to swallow everything

Under this azure blanket and green carpet.

What a charming thing it would be

For these leaves to turn orange and yellow

And dry, trampled golden under our feet.

Seasons have stopped changing.

Predictability, repetition, and monotony

Seem to devour us—

All living in patches inside a mason jar,

Cleanly convoluted and humdrum

Like a control group of mice

Being examined with sophistication,

All ready to be tested

For their mental agility,

Hoarding emotional resilience!

Death of a Spider in Times of Social Distancing

Written under lockdown in a forest at the border between Ethiopia and Sudan.

You do not know what excites you anymore.

That mundane life of your heroic deeds

Crowded with sham accolades and attire.

That mundane life of being swallowed into riddles,

Tightly clasping its jaws,

Not knowing if you are the puzzle

Or your grandiose commitment to others.

That mundane life of making long commutes

On rowdy lanes to undefined destinations.

It was all taken away

At the press of a button: *Shut Down*.

The gods played a maverick joke on humanity—

"Killing a few" versus "weaponizing all,"

As if, in the checkerboard game of life,

We lost a bet.

What a divine strategy!

Pregnant with self-control,

Patience, and introspection.

That you die, not because of

Your lack of self-worth,

But because of your partner's dissidence.

Suddenly, all those childhood nicknames

Flash in front of your eyes,

Replaying like a movie about to come to a standstill.

Are we going back to square one

Of why we were created in the first place?

To enrich oneself, maybe—

But to enrich for the common good

And common good alone.

For a life is worthy

When it makes others' lives worthy.

Death of a spider on my shower floor

Was merely a testimony

Of its mortality!

Not in the Audience

I never had to struggle

To learn about diversity,

To learn a new language,

To learn how to breathe—

Strangled, cramped up in a metro,

Surrounded by men.

I never had to protest

Against the newly found

Injustice,

Misogyny,

Corruption,

Bigotry,

Racism—

None of that.

I never had to volunteer

To experience culture shock.

To see pain in faraway places

Down to the South

And a bit of the North,

But south of the South,

Mostly.

To see suffering in shoddy huts,

Dilapidated buildings,

Mangroves flooded with mud

And alligators,

A man cremating himself

Because of a lack of identity

From his government,

A man devouring the corpse

Like vultures, but much worse,

A woman bleeding quarts

And blood smeared all over her cotton rags.

I never had to struggle

To see how misrepresentation

Leads to faux leadership.

How democracy sits wreathed in smoke

And wallows in the compartments

Of each and every broken track

Of a railway station.

Basically,

How a nation gets auctioned

For sugar

And how tears become

Cheaper than onions.

How a name could save your life

But destroy a clan.

I never had to struggle to see

All of this—

The perks

Of being on stage,

Not in the audience!

Watch
Me
Burn

A Girl Who Reads

Across the shores of the Libyan coast,

On the dangerous waters of the Mediterranean,

In the deserted lanes of Kunduz,

Into the smuggled alleys of Cox's Bazaar,

There is a common spirit of change

That breeds

To change systems of education

And builds

To change systems of forced marriages and guilt.

Because in the age of atrocities

Against opinions and thoughts

Beyond ethnicities and borders,

Nothing sucks worse than a girl who reads.

I say this because

A girl who reads possesses a vocabulary.

A vocabulary

That can describe the discontents of life.

A vocabulary that parses the innate need for education

And makes it a necessity instead of a privilege.

Because a girl who reads understands words—

Words that flow with rhythm

Like musical notes of life—

A life well-lived.

Literature has taught her

That moments of triumph come in sporadic intervals

Because a girl who reads

Is aware

That life is not a Disneyland,

Filled with charms and magic.

She rightly understands

That the ebb comes along with the flow of disappointments.

Because a girl who reads

Comprehends the difference

Between a moment of anger and abuse

And the habits of bitter traditions.

Because a girl who reads

Knows the importance of a plot.

She knows significance of an end.

And

She is comfortable with it

Because a girl who reads can weave a life

Bursting with meaning.

She insists that her narratives are rich

And will not accept a life less than passion,

Perfection—

A life worthy of being written into story.

Because, you see,

The girls who read

Are thinkers!

They will compare you with the likes of

Rumi, Tolstoy, and Khaled Hosseini!

That's when—that's when

A voice comes roaring across the border

Amidst intense shelling,

Pregnant with rebuke and assault:

You, girl, get lost! Take the next train!

I hate you. I really, really hate you.

Because you are the girl who reads!

Making of a Unicorn

You bashed me left, right, and center,

Choked my mouth.

I begged for civility

And respect.

You took my silence for weakness,

As I defended my case,

Confounded in a room

Filled with utter chaos

And allegations.

Confounded in a room

Filled with utter imbalance—

The power imbalance.

You tripped me so many times.

I was wounded

In so many

Places and ways

That I stopped caring enough

To wipe off the blood.

And you still wonder

How I turned into a unicorn?

Woman of Color

So she responded:

I am not *trying* to be different.

I *am* different.

It is your problem that you can't see

Beyond my color,

Race, creed, and sex,

Language, fingers, and toes.

You must get creative.

May you peruse through

The books I wrote,

The words I spoke,

The friendships I forged,

The communities I served

To discover a deeper meaning

In the life I lived.

Containment

Sometimes I can't contain this world.

Sometimes it can't contain me.

The more often the latter happens,

The more I become China.

It seems like a betrayal—

A New Silk Road

On the rise.

So go ahead—

Applaud my wounds,

Jeer and boast

At my downfall.

After all,

It's not so uncommon.

Even the sun goes down

Every day.

Watch Me Burn

*Dedicated to the wildfires
in Australia, January 2020.*

In your quest to know yourself more,

I dare to reveal the toughest truths of all.

Go chase and connect

With that which connects these burning trees

And their crimson leaves,

The blood-laden skies of the utter south,

These rivers emitting indispensable fury

To vibrations of the wilderness.

Absorb.

Watch them have this incredible faith

In their restoration and rebirth,

In their sudden demise and its worth.

Watch them grow in the darkest of ages.

I say to you: Go watch how stars rise,

Unfailingly devising their needs each night,

Only waiting to die

One more time

With a sore belief

That I am enough—

Always will be.

But your glory makes it worthy.

Born a Debt

When you're born a woman—

A woman in the third world,

A woman in this world,

A woman with light nationality,

A woman with bold personality,

A woman with no work,

A woman with so much turf,

A woman too divine,

An atheist too beguiling,

A woman with no pen,

A woman with no men,

A woman who cannot step out,

Who cannot step up,

A woman too young,

A woman a bit old,

A woman too beautiful,

A woman less bold,

A woman in love,

A woman of color—

Your existence

Is impugned

Each day

By uncles and aunts,

By doctors and teachers,

By guards and fiends,

By home and state,

By life and its minions.

You're a woman

Born a debt

And, to some, an asset

In disguise!

Floating on the Wings of Faith

One thousand things happened—

None to my liking.

So now I am confident

The universe must be in love—

Like *really* in love—

With me!

A Miniscule Familiarity with Danger

Every time I look into your eyes—

Halt! Don't romanticize!—

A minuscule familiarity strikes.

Why I couldn't initiate a conversation?

In the hinterlands of strangeness,

Familiarity is a scary phenomenon.

I never tried finding out—

Who are you? What are you?

All the lands you walked,

All the rivers you ventured,

All the mountains you wished,

All the karma you earned.

It's not OK to be so familiar.

A minuscule familiarity—

It is unsettling.

It is dangerous.

The little I know—your story—

You aspire to realistic dreams

Of unsettling me.

But I chase dreamy realism,

Separated like the banks of the Zambezi

That will never meet,

That are still real,

That still dream.

One more time, I recede

To ensnare you in full light.

One more time, I walk away.

But the familiarity perturbs.

So I wonder:

Who are you?

Why are you?

I am scared.

The little I know—your story—

Of your triumphs and heartbreaks,

Of your journey and masquerades,

Of your toils and wishes,

Reminds me of a past I lived.

So now you know what

The addiction means.

It's not infatuation; it's not dedication.

It's not attraction; it's not blind adoration.

It's striking familiarity!

Familiarity is a noise.

I want it ceased!

Your every invitation to the ball is struck dead,

Left bereft in the court.

So I play fair one last time.

How could one value something without knowing its value?

I want to know you—

You, danger—

So the familiarity exists!

Receded, I stand still.

No bargain can be struck

To appease the noise.

The past does matter, especially

When it drains the present.

But if you knew mine,

The same familiarity would strike

And you'd be scared too!

Feast on Me, Afrika!

The manacles on my wrists are bludgeons;
The choker round my neck, forged as a shield.
Come and feast, Afrika!

Doe-eyed spears glow in every river's marsh,
Sharper than ever before,
More painful than Karen Blixen's sacrifice.
The inky night, ruddy with the enemy's blood.
The Mara River, a stench abode of defeated knuckles,
Flooded by your Great Migration,
Meant for wildebeests, not humans.
Or did you forget, Afrika?

Come dance, Afrika!
In your spirit of demolition, with ease,
Stop to feast on your sons and daughters
Like your heroes did with the English

And the French and the Portuguese.

But dance with me, Afrika!

Your rivers that were swollen with alligators,

Today, are docile with infant bodies,

With the crimson drapes of teenager's unwanted gestations.

Your men have languished their fire into shame,

Resolving to cowardice,

Sometimes by raping or being raped,

Hiding in the dark crevices of Kilimanjaro.

Come forth, Afrika!

Beat back your wildness,

Levied in the formidable pauses of Madiba's stride.

The earth's beats are aligning in me,

Dancing like flying shrapnel in war.

So now, I am Afrika, too—

A woman fashioned in your shape.

I am you, and my gait

Reflects your leonine stride.

Come forth, Afrika!

Come strike out like a lion,

So we can gauge

If you can actually feast on me.

The Corporate Jungle: A Memoir to Skyscrapers in Tokyo

Hearken to the tale of serendipities,

The perplexities of these towering desires,

Crowding humanitarian zoos,

Fatal destinies torn between limbs and elbows.

The intensity of the metaphysics of this city

Blinds the dainty pedestrians of Shinjuku San-Chome,

Bewildering shapes and gothic faces filling Harajuku.

So we ask ourselves, collectively in sync:

What was brilliantly revealed

In the flamboyant aspirations of Kabukicho,

In the underground dungeons of Don Quijote,

Caged in capsule hotel dreams?

Neither Namba district's mirror reflections

Nor Roppongi's celestial beauty remained.

With what caliber should I count my indifferences?
Desire akin to a hundred goblets of wine brimming,
Yet, in the vessel of the heart, silence remained.

What a marvelous instance it was
When I tasted the elixir of defiance,
Questioning the fundamentals of happiness
And the corporate ladder it is all built on.
So I ran in stilettos, metro to metro,
Digging my heels in deep trenches of homogeneity.
I ran inside Shinkansen, chasing cloudy capitalism,
Passing by a queue of shinbun readers on my left,
All reading a book of reason undusted on a shelf.
On the shelf, it remained.

A whirlpool from the threshold blew unseen
Between my sticky fingers,
Soaked in the sake of bliss,
All so dreadfully consumed.

Yet a branch on the tree of sorrow called Kokoro,
Green, it remained.
The samurai of divinity bestowed upon me
The purple robes of nudity.
Neither the stitching of caution
Nor the veils of madness remained.

Neither the ardor of hope
Nor the celestial soul remained.
Neither did you nor I remain.
Only an unspoken awareness remained.

The fire of serendipity has reduced the mute hearts to ashes.
Neither fright nor caution remained,
In the stories of Nippon.
Only fearlessness remained.

Reading in Rage, Writing in Tranquility

The way some men piercingly gaze,

As though they see some sort of exotic animal

Caged in an arctic zoo,

Chills my bones

And steams my nerves.

C'mon, let me read my newspaper.

Let me have my cup of cappuccino.

That air of unsolicited authority,

That whiff of cigar that passes your vanity—

Keep it to yourself.

Tightly embalmed, I am

With sterile indifference.

Don't mess with it.

I might read in rage,

But I write in tranquility.

Secret Admirers of Feminism

So appalling

Is your abundance—

Is your silence—

Is your stillness—

The ways you inject yourself

Or crave to be injected

With my bloodless stream of feminism—

With its deciduous power to convey—

With its seething presence to thrive—

Often so desirably that

You forget the reason of its existence.

So I, as the curator

Of this art,

Urge you to see beyond

The mere beauty and margins

And, if time

And place allow,

Try to rip it apart—

All the layers

And all the glumness.

For what lacks in your admirations

Is a black woman's heroism

That knows when to be bold

When to be humble!

Women and Confidence

Sometimes I wish we never became friends.

Good that we did.

Sometimes I wish I hadn't been dismantled.

Good that I was.

Sometimes I wish you were that crown

We could hang onto,

But not all diamonds can be clasped.

Sometimes I wish you resisted us all vehemently,

But you always saved us mysteriously

In the ways I did not like.

Sometimes I wish I could understand

Our friendship so much better—

What it is and what it is not—

But I can't!

What a destitute place to be in, you may say.

So I run out of water—

Water of patience and seeds of ignorance.

So masochistic, you say.

But that's the law of nature.

Even roses cherish the company of thorns,

So why should we regret yours?

But still I can't understand our friendship.

For now, I don't hate you enough

To turn my exposé into fame

Or to go down the rabbit hole each day and conjecture

What a gorgeous friend you are, confidence!

Resilience

You want to find me.

Seems like a long time.

You're wearing a crown

Behind a frazzled crowd.

Standing right by you,

You will find me!

In the Best of Fall, I Rise

In the best of rise—

Audacious clamors,

Desperate neighs,

And fictitious banners—

I pray when you fall,

You fall with grace,

In gratitude and honesty.

For there's no greater high

Than living in the nascent truth

Of distinguished palates—

Tiny feet,

A jar of milk,

Morsels of laughter.

I rise, in the best of fall,

In the summery fragrance of chalice vines

And the underused comforts of docile mortality!

Discourses with Fear

Now I know you more.

Now I know you better.

If you hadn't jumped off the cliff,

How would I know you could fly?

It would be a mere speculation,

Sour so much time.

That's exactly what you don't have.

Thank goodness, now I know

That you can fly!

There's beauty that rests

On the wings of dismay and solitude.

There's calmness that reigns

That could make you flightless,

But you fly for the sake of it.

For how will you know the heights that exist?

Within you and without,

In the desert.

So fly for the sake of it.

Many seasons will come and go,

But many may not climb with you.

The cliff from which you jumped

This time

Will remain forever the best time

Because that's when you came to know

You could fly.

You could fly too!

Why is there a battle of wills?

I do not understand.

But you still found your wings

And I still write this muse.

So when you approach the cliff

One more time,

It will echo. It will linger.

Phantasmagoria

In my book of travelogues

Hides a page on contemplations—

Contemplations on immortality,

On fear and courage,

On butterflies and pessimism,

On lows and highs,

On celibacy and eroticism.

Enclosed in the book of colorful hesitancies,

Enclosed in the book of a thousand assumptions,

I fly on.

Just a mention of its name—

Whenever mentioned—

And the book is inflamed in fireballs,

Fireballs with the fragrance of wastelands.

In those wastelands, I chirp. I get intoxicated,

Enraptured in its phantasmagoria.

What is this phantasmagoria?
Neither my heart knows nor my gaze.
With the endless trails unfolding in front of me,
I take off again on the wheels of fire,
Rustling through the heat of Zanzibar,
Merging into the turquoise waters of Ile aux Cerfs,
Dancing to the beats of the upside-down trees,
Unwinding on the coastline of Seychelles.

I take off to hear the whispers
Passing through the mysticism of Lake Baikal.
That's when its neon light perforates my skin,
Piercing silhouettes of untouched terrains,
All imploring me to stay!

But I run again to chase tranquility,
Chased by this travelogue,
Chased by the phantasmagoria of its phantoms,
Estranged by them all, but still I race
Against everything known and flimsy,
Against the graveness of shams and egotism,

Towards gravestones' solemn tranquility.

Tranquility that rests in the Blue Grotto of Capri.
Tranquility that revels in the Lake Palace of Udaipur.
Tranquility that rushes in the breezes of the trulli.
Tranquility that speaks to the backwaters of Kerala.
The same tranquility dies at a writer's desk.

Tranquility that shrieks in the middle of my nights,
Through the starlit sky of the equator,
A sky that blazes into the northern lights of Iceland.
Tranquility that rests on the ashes floating on the Ganges
And which blends in the colors of Cinque Terre.
Tranquility that gushes in the Milk Grotto of Bethlehem,
Which roars through the mountains of Calvary.
The same tranquility silently hangs
In the village of Montbovon
On the divinely carved doors of St. Grat!

But I take off again.
I race through the world below me,

Around me, and in me,

Far away from this dampening zoo—

Miles away from the fists of artificialities,

Miles away from the feigned cheers of debauchery,

Miles away from the twisted shackles of capitalism.

Lo! I float on the whimsical clouds, soft as smoke,

Touched gently—all gushing to dampen my soul

Through the Black Forest on the foggy Rhine,

Enticed by the white rocks of the Sossusvlei dunes,

Dining at the Palace on Wheels,

Finessing at the coffee tables of Al Andalus.

Like a dream running parallel,

Royalty touches them both.

No matter how much I dust it away,

It still sticks to me.

Dust that shimmers, gleams, and pervades,

Inviting only connivers and mercenaries

To lurk around my chalice of amicability,

With sips so tempting and reactions so cagey,

At the very sight of it running dry,

I run over the alarming tracks of the Serengeti,

Like a gazelle escaping crocodiles.

I fly again—

Sometimes from stone to stone,

Sometimes from leaf to leaf.

If only Dante had left a cup undrunk,

I would cherish it at the Trevi Fountain.

I care not if I race against untiring walls of spite.

I care not if his inferno burns me to ashes.

I care not if St. Anastasia of Verona lit one extra candle.

I care not if Shakespeare sketched graffiti on Giulietta's wall.

All I care is that I will be there to smell

The coffee when it's brewed—

A coffee that will transcend my world!

But the quest alone will not matter.

This existence will not matter.

There arc boundless phantasmagorias

That exist beyond this land and sea.

Phantasmagoria of ultimate truth.

Phantasmagoria of no facades or illusions.

Dare not cease, O travelogue!

There are more paradises to explore.

Dreams within will grow shoots of doubt, so then

Dare not fall seasick within sight of the shore.

Dare not cease, even upon the loss of one abode.

There are a million addresses to claim

That glitter in the form of stars and fame.

I never fell for any of them.

No scenery so beautiful cajoled me,

Nor will I ever stop.

I discovered the worldly chasms too early.

Now I rest on demure clouds.

But you are a falcon, my travelogue!

Do not rest in the oasis unclaimed.

Do not take refuge in the mirages of royalty.

Do not lose yourself in the cycles of days and nights.

Remember: your passion is flight!

Spread your wings once again and
Soar higher than before,
For you have more skies to transcend.
Do not rest, O falcon of the travelogue!

With no regrets or exigencies,
Suddenly, all the cities, hamlets, towers, and bridges,
The souls breathing through them,
Their talks about minds and hearts,
The architecture and its ingenuity—
All look the same.

All deceitful, all illusionary,
All numbing, all indifferent,
All unsympathetic to this travelogue.
All unaware of their own pursuits.
So how would they know yours?
So care not, O travelogue!
But fly once again!

Sedation of a Vision

Rose petals shedding in my kitchen

On a glass and granite slab

With reflections as clear as a mirror.

I see them shed so fast,

Faster than a funeral wreath.

Roses, O dear, you blind my sight

And my vision, even more often.

So I trick myself into being sedated—

Sedated by your thorns

To keep my sight real

And my vision reborn.

Café of Humbleness

In search of humbleness,

I'm smoking long-held loyalties—

Facades all demolished

And music unheard.

My search widens one more time

For a smell so intoxicating,

So translucent but defining that,

Every time I visualize myself

Passing through your doors,

I am sweetened in a desert

That cultivates no sugar!

Galloping chariots of such dreams

Must halt at this café,

Or so I presume.

I lack desire to chase them,

To take their reins.

What have you made of me?

Lo! Humbleness!

You levitate like untouched clouds.

Now all I can do is

Wait for you to rain on me

In a desert that cultivates no sugar!

Ancestral Tribute

Amongst all the messages I sent out,

There were none so grave

So as to hold you back on this mortal Earth.

Yet in the twilight hours of this day,

I envy the flames

That wrapped around you

Like cozy blankets of triumph and tranquility.

I envy how they rose and shimmered,

Your camphoric lips glistening like an angel

Shining through a soiled wreath,

Each plume rising from the ashes

Like a golden rite of passage—

A passage I didn't ask for.

So ghastly, I stood on the porch gazing at your pyre,

Envying how they smiled in embracing you,

Willfully and nonchalantly

Tasting your heart,

Stealing my prerogative,

Smashed into tiny pieces of diamond

Glowing like fireflies in the sea of time,

Celebrating an infinite void created between you and me!

Chastity Test

I am just a bit less

Than your words of praise

And just a bit more

Than an hourglass.

But if you absolutely must summarize,

I say, summarize me

In your heart.

It'll save you rocks,

Paper,

And scissors.

Mimosa Stories Retold

There is one you drink

And there is one you aspire to be.

To be or not to be

Is the question.

It has always been!

Let's accept that

Because

Mimosas never lied—

Not a single slip of the tongue,

Not a single slice of orange,

Not a single plunge

Ever ruined

Or wasted

Already-devastated souls.

Mimosas only gave words

To pre-existing thoughts

Each time they were injected

Into my bloodstream—

Or yours.

Because—

Let's be honest—

Mimosas often know the price

You paid before drinking

And not after.

Yet no one asks the price

You paid

In the process!

Synonyms for Happiness

Look how you recede

From the tenterhooks

Of my preponderance,

Unclipped from the lanyard

Of my conscience,

In the backyard

Of my neighborhood.

And that was

Heartening enough

To keep me disillusioned,

So I could seek synonyms.

Synonyms for happiness—

Not a necessity,

But a profusely

Coveted

Human guilt

That we aim to hide

And so often

Wish to commit!

Learn to Pick Your Price

Not everyone can pay the price of a diamond.

Some will call it a rock.

Some will label it "a piece of glass."

But the diamond does not despair.

It waits for the day to shine

In the hands of a true patron.

That's when heads turn.

That's when they fade away in awe!

Perspectives

On a spinning wheel of Sahel,

I spin cotton, day and night.

Threads of desires and their besotted dreams,

Of persuasions and fragile guilt,

Of quagmires and their strangled knots,

Of perspectives on which they are all built.

In the loneliness of the deserted wilderness,

Do not wander, O naïve heart!

Even upon deprivation of all the water and rain,

Do not run like a thirsty wave in its own river.

Do not flutter like a bird in a cage.

Do not glimmer like a mermaid hidden.

Do not wrestle like a loose plume in the wind.

Yet as I spin cotton under the night lamp,

What pulsates you in every direction?

Utter not, until I speak.

You dream of unheard lands and seas,

Of unseen mezzanines and divine paths,

Of cryptic languages that utter truth

And paths stuck in their own ways.

Of blinding shades and mirror-like talks,

Of their piercing sound as they fall.

Of unscathed swords and relinquished thrones,

Of a silent perspective that controls them all.

As you step closer on the road untaken,

May your strides be firmer than before,

Your convictions steadier than the wind,

Your speech gentler than rose petals,

Your nerves conscious of a thousand hints.

So when you carry them on your fatigued shoulders,

You will know that you are not alone.

Encircling you are walls and chaste cages

And every bar that bifurcates them all,

From religion to class distinction.

I call them borders, but you call them perspectives!

Kotoba

Let my words shatter into tiny pieces

Of stoic courage,

Such that they inspire hope

In the youth and the downtrodden.

Let them shimmer in the minds of the bereaved

And those craving justice.

But if they cannot be a balm for the discouraged—

My words—may they die in silence.

For it may be unfortunate,

But not as unfortunate

As leaving a corpse even more dead.

Mental Health

How come I miss the presence

Of calmness?

It's not like it was ever present

Or tactile,

But that's the only way

I know

How to turn dreams

Into reality!

Finding a Muse

I used to teach painting.

Some painted in watercolor,

Some in oil.

Some tortured tons of gold,

Some burned down the foil.

But those who painted none of these

Often sought new techniques

Through pencils and pens,

Inks and charcoal—

Too brittle,

Too loose.

But I often wondered

Why I couldn't teach about how to spot

A muse!

No Wonder Rumi Fell in Love So Easily!

Be careful whom you fall in love with—
Not because it has the capacity to shatter you,
But because it has the power to lift you up
So much closer to the skies above
And the divinity they hold.
So much closer to the ethereal beauty of God.
Not the type nested on cascades of taffeta,
Chiffon bows, and ostrich feathers,
Depicting Romanesque frescos on gala dresses.
No wonder Rumi fell in love so easily—
Ruminating on the aphrodisiac of loyalty,
Filled with the cadence of a bliss-point trust.
Commitment—a potent high—
Is often more romantic than romance.
So exercise it with caution.
Be careful whom you allow to wield that power
Over you.
Be careful whom you choose to rise with.

La Couleur Du Sang

Don't you see how much in love I am with you, that

I'm painting you blue,

In the color of my beloved country, Sudan?

I'm painting crimson for the daffodils

Left on the table by Van Gogh's introspections

And the spears for the conscience.

I'm painting disarray for your perturbed, trembling heart.

I'm painting yellow for the bloodstreams,

Hollowness for the faith—

Whichever scriptures you believe in.

Suddenly mesmerized by the illusions

Created by two languages of Ambazonia,

Questing at the borderlines of Bamenda,

I'm painting violet

For Anglophones

And their nascent history.

So how can my love be any lesser

Than these colors of human blood

And the virility of it?

It is blue as we live.

It is red as we weep.

It is white as we try to save it.

That's what makes it English!

A Library Kind of Love

Brew me a library

Scintillating in its every page

With all its effervescence,

Tantalizing with thoughts

Of euphony and moral compass.

A love so tender—

A library

Of utter solace and serenity,

Floating like a pair of swans on a deserted lake.

Brew me a canyon of impeccable modesty,

Drifting in the air like balloons in Cappadocia Valley.

Brew me a river dazzling with vintage symphony

Of skies preaching stars and dancing waves.

Brew me the breeze of lavender farms

Inside this library

Of indefinite murmurings,

Faltering landscapes of manmade tempers,

Doting eyes of a novel that never ends.

Brew me a library of a different kind,

Fuming with passion and knowledge,

That dissolves in hot water

Like the pages so incomplete,

And absorbs every bit of it

Like a potion so neat!

Zanzibari Rhapsody: A Feline Encounter

I passed you on a sunny day

On a dingy corner of Zanzibar,

Through lanes as narrow as test tubes,

Inhaling the smoky piscine flavors

Flowing through my chest and into my ribs,

As if, all at once, we were one in body and spirit—

Which Freddie would call: *such a Queen act.*

Incubating my soul in a rough patch

And yours—oh, well—yours—

Not a hairsbreadth of sympathy for the mortals

Bereaved in a solo excursion of beggary,

Drenched in the hollow faith of my kindness.

I pursue you so you don't pursue me.

Behind these dark cloudy skies falls the giant Old Fort,

With shadows of a coliseum that resurrects itself over moss.

An unsettling stature,

As if poaching traditions out of me in small doses,
As if to compensate for the normalcy they all desire
But which they hardly manage to garner.
I begin to think of you and those alike
And how you suffer in this heat of untamed desires
Between phantoms of Kigomani circle
And their deluded fishermen baskets.
How incomprehensible it must be
To lie over the rooftops on a cloudy day,
With the not-so-symphonic traffic noise
That pierces through the dilapidated glass of an old mosque,
Ruined on one side by some tragic influx
Of the Russian parade
And on the other by a masquerade of clumsy tourists.
So I pursue you, so you don't pursue me!

An Affair with Thoughts

Me, in the corner of a café,

Crafting an intoxicating brew of honeycombed

Thoughts—

It's the best-kept secret in the world.

Oh, how I delight in them!

How poorly I drown in them.

How gracefully they embrace me.

How whimsically we adore

The space in me

And the beauty in you.

How sacred is this sacrament.

I'd rather be in this corner

Alone

Than anywhere else!

Moringa Enlightenments

Written under lockdown in a forest at the border between Ethiopia and Sudan, in search of divinity.

So while I sit to cherish these mangroves,

The abandoned Kigelia africana of this desert,

These works of mine,

Their surreal overnight becoming,

They both sit under Moringa shades

To contemplate

In solemn disgrace and herculean apathy

Whether these works of mine

Are concrete,

Riddle-free, and just,

Whether they bear fruits for generations.

If so, where do they take me?

So I sit contemplating

To use a voice so loud,

Clear like miniature diamonds in white sands,

Piercingly shining, saying:

You cannot be truer to me than I.

You cannot be fairer to me than I.

You cannot be more loving to you than I.

For I approached you before

You could even approach me!

Stop and Smell the Roses!

At the age of seventeen, I was told:

Expectation is the root cause of all heartache.

And while that is true,

I haven't stopped giving my best.

I haven't stopped to smell the roses.

I haven't stopped at all—

Not because I am expecting

More from others,

But because I am expecting

More from myself.

I think that's legit!

My Polish Grill

In my desire to understand
The ubiquitous friendships of our age
That flow from one electric charge to another
Like pendulums dropped from the leaning tower
In acute mayhem—
Challenging both gravity and Galileo's assumptions—
I was once invited to a Polish grill,
Where kielbasa was a necessity
And guzzling firewater down the throat, a rite of passage.
Where folklore was mentioned in sweetness
And women's rights went sumptuously unaddressed.
Where chicken had wings, melting profusely in our bellies,
Seeking unsaid redemption
From the ungodly journeys they made
Through charcoal pits to our hungry souls.
Feeding friendships
That rose like the great waves of Kanagawa,
Trespassing on our walls and dreams,
Glittering under the roofless sky of Van Gogh's *Starry Night*.
I was once invited to a Polish grill!

Characterization of a Unicorn

Here's the thing: it's good to dress in a thousand shades

Of sham glamour,

In Balenciaga boots catered to Seychelles beach days,

Like flamingoes adorned in pink fluff,

Only to lure the most timid

At soirées that serve caviar of poignant flavors

Diffusing into nose, ears, and mouth

As if by osmosis.

A cause of bronchitis,

Inhaling can be work, especially the misogynist molecules

Only unicorns managed to survive.

It's easy to wonder what's real.

And while it is good to dress in a thousand shades

Of sham glamour,

Nothing is as dignifying as the character itself—

A character that is a confit of fluffy dreams and humanity,

Which lacks muscles of racism and mischaracterization,

Which colors the vibgyor

With truth and intensity,

With kindness and elitism,

With modesty and perseverance.

No golden dust can overpower that.

Take the character out of the confit

And all you get is blandness.

Time to walk my unicorn. Sorry to drop this call!

A Tiger's Shadow

Like a beguiling tiger

Ravenous to hunt his dreams

In the cool dark shades of Ranthambore

Amidst a train of elapsed regal memories,

Gradually positioning himself

Again to pounce,

Claws of faith ready to clutch.

Bravery washes his stripes,

Watching his shadow being swallowed

From a distance

By a long-held belief that says:

Some days I stand out

For reasons so cherished.

Other days I'm out of this world.

And those days, as I recall, are

Every day!

From the Ashes

Mermaid Dreams for a Decade

Forlorn causes and desperate shows

Dissembled all for once

Like in an aquatic amusement, the mermaid shrinks her fins

To hope for

A little more than today.

For the slumber is over!

Gone are the days

And what a decade it has been.

She dreams again—

Can't wait to swim into 2021

Wildly and gently as always!

Rise of a New Decade

Behold my rays—

How seductively they rise,

Getting high on a decade,

Claiming

Destiny has brought me to you.

You're already changing my fate,

Hoping I will change yours too.

So when you retreat into the acute

Solace of the night,

May you retrospect in peace,

Like a golden leaf of history

Turning the page to a new era.

Because what has ended is the present.

What is beginning now is the future!

A Bullish Feminism

Soon everyone shall be feminist,

Said the fearless girl.

Soon we will have rights

Handed to us like candies!

But the charging bull felt entitled.

He barraged—

In the 1910s, against the voice to vote;

In the 1920s, he stomped at equal education;

In the 1960s, against equal wage.

But after a few drooping decades,

Nothing much changed.

She yelled:

We want equal pay!

Not to berate you,

Not to steal your share of the pie,

Not to abhor you,

But because

I work one night the same as you.

I work one day the same as you.

On a spinning wheel of Sahel,

I spin cotton the same as you—

Threads of desires

And their besotted dreams,

Of persuasions

And fragile egos,

Of quagmires

And their strangled ambitions—

To build a legacy

The same as you!

So no, Hunter-mind!

It is not one more plot to hatch,

Not one more plague to cure,

Definitely

Not one more mystery to solve.

But the bull wasn't convinced;

He charged—

With words and actions,

With knees and elbows,

With the deluged and disillusioned

Egos.

So, said the fearless girl,

Please continue.

I must feel your fear.

Fear is important.

Don't take that away.

In order to believe

In your ruckus stories,

In your unearned pride,

In your swathed ingenuity,

Fear is important.

Don't take that away.

Just don't.

But remember,

When you lift your bullish weight alone,

You shall know the price of rice old,

The price of masculinity, and the price of gold,

Because

Encircling you will be the white sands and the brown,

The Blue Nile and the White.

And with every grain that drifts apart,

A grueling anonymity will bifurcate them all

From education to sexuality.

You call it tradition, but I call it legacy!

Womanned Up!

*A tribute to the courage of
Dr. Christine Blasey Ford.*

In a world full of women,

I often wonder:

Why don't men speak up?

Woman up!

And speak up!

Why don't men speak up?

When "locker-room talk"

Is not consent.

When beyond "having coffee"

Is not consent.

When securing sexual education

Is not consent.

When in marital contention

Is not consent.

When not awake

Is not consent.

When wearing makeup

Is not consent.

When lack of due process

Encourages anarchy.

But how would I know?

Dear Dr. Blasey Ford,

It's still a man's world

Where you womanned up!

Solitary Hope

As I look up and sigh

At the descending branches of this acacia tree

Against the shimmering backdrop of a glowing moon,

I am belligerently reminded of the stillness

In the air

And its unsung symphonies and discourses.

I am belligerently struck by the undying faith in faith.

How discouraging it must be to shine all night

Only to be forgotten the next day!

Blessings of the Eighth of March

Trampled by the bustling wind

And rain in the course of an hour,

Bottlebrush spread over a mile,

Covering the aisles of a gloomy street.

No sweet lilies or damsel roses.

No sweet peonies or floundering mustard.

I'm a sweet stock girl

Of a purple type.

Prune me some classic blooms tonight!

Albeit this may be your last night

Of blessings,

Of untouched miracles.

So have a blessed night tonight!

Urvashi Bundel

Pashmina Thoughts

When your dreams overpower your intuition.
When the night suffers insomnia in disguise
And a frail alley into the forest beckons more often
Than any rational trails of dynasties and their pedigrees.
When Dasht-e-Abdan glistens like a mirage
Crowning the meadows of Kunduz,
Lost in the fumes of bones and ashes.
Compelling humanity to weave and
Embroider its badges of disingenuous fame,
Stitch knightly collars for its warlords
With the vulnerable threads of pashmina—
Entangled in our beliefs and the ones we break,
Entwined with our religions
And the miseries we encore to it.
Pashmina thoughts are docile,
Delicate, and fragile,
Yet stronger than any tyrant's
Dalliance and discourse!

Howling: Times of Isolation

Written under lockdown in a forest at the border between Ethiopia and Sudan.

I hear wolves howl in the dark of this night,

A diffident white owl hooting,

Perched on impoverished branches of Sodom.

A snail crawls down through dingy thickets and shrubs

And hissing of a serpent silences the howl.

Unhindered, the bamboo forest grows large and tall,

Preaching tenacity to those who fall,

Spreading its embrace wider and wider.

And so can we, by ourselves and all.

Science of Humanities

If you ever wondered why humanities don't use numbers,

Ask a journalist speculating foreign policy

Based on the colors of ties

And the starchiness of the premier handshakes.

If you ever thought measuring time was for scientists,

Ask a barrister defending a war-torn child,

Meticulously recording the chronology of her journey—

A journey of tears

Running furiously from Raqqa to Cúcuta,

From the demystified roofs of Mosul

To the dark crevices of unsung Rakhine.

But if you ever wondered whether scales were for architects,

Ask a poet

Who measures the ebb and flow of his every syllable,

Charming the pages to efface mysticism

As and when required, wisely enough

To shelter and martyr every letter

In utter unison, all in the name of humanity!

Legacy

What if tomorrow you came to know

There was something more than gravity

That was holding us to this Earth?

What if feeding others was the only currency?

Would you still be of worth?

And if all that mattered was

Self-worth,

What makes you think the legacy would stay

Upon your passage

Under the soil?

Make It Count

The land where clouds cast shadows

So indelible and indefinite,

As if mapping a civilization of their own

With differences and distance.

As I land,

They make me fortify

An unswerving thought:

There's not much to this world.

Not much to it.

Not much to the time spent.

But while you're at it,

Make it count!

At Church, Every Single Day!

If ever you had time to cry over

Lost defenses,

Cherished friendships,

And unhinged fences.

If ever you had time to comprehend

Words as they are written

And not how you expect them to be,

Disease as it is

And not how you wish it would disappear.

If ever you had time to demand

Justice for a downtrodden soul

And put off fire, glaring

In the face of fear.

If ever you were

So privileged,

You'd be at home

At church

Every single day!

Circumcised Halos

Isn't it confusing when meeting

Celebrities?

When you don't know if you should celebrate them

Or what they stand for?

When you don't know if you should believe in their art

Or the reasons they support it?

But what I do know is that,

When I meet any, especially the ones

With circumcised halos,

I know they have a power to create constructive dialogue

Among the most malnourished minds

And souls.

So then I wonder what should I celebrate:

Their keenness to shine

Or the shine they promise in others?

A Cinderella Hour

Obfuscate the delusional symptoms of apathy

In your heart of hearts—

Make it stay, make it home.

Mirror, O mirror!

May the mirror be your guide.

Let me stay in this Cinderella hour

Between twilight and dusk.

Not everyone wears crystal-glass shoes

Designed to consume grandiosity.

Dance with me on these mirrors,

Crushing every image that's unreal.

Dance with your ballerinas,

For many a toe has bled on this floor.

Make it stay, make it home, Cinderella.

After all, how many castles do you get

In this lifetime

That won't vanish at the break of a spell,

At the break of the dawn?

So make it stay, make it home!

When Dreaming Is an Urgency

I see them run like giants in the hallways of Wall Street.

I see them churn a stupendous hour into gold,

Drooping within seconds.

Each breathing down their necks

Like a landmine unstepped-upon,

In their brogues and wigs

And dirt all around,

With reined horses unkempt.

I see men hoping for a peaceful harvest,

But rain is also a season.

Most days we protect our parade.

But when urgency strikes

At the core of our existence—

Our survival

And its immediate depletion—

We take bold steps

To dream of a thousand dreams,

Of a thousand pathways

Leading to one single moment.

So dream relentlessly today

Because, if there's any moment that'll stay,

It is this one!

A Soliloquy for Libra Season

Dedicated to world-famous Libra, Mahatma Gandhi, on the occasion of his 150th Birthday anniversary.

Words, you see, I've acquired them in heritage

For the worst of times and days.

So seldom they rise from the depths of our throats,

The louder they sound from the epiglottis of our rage.

I know it is hard to imagine a world with scales so balanced

That no day in Libra season surpass them—

That my egalitarian dreams are satisfied overnight.

But yet I see you watching from the sidelines

For this magic to be unveiled

And yet I see you take no action.

What a waste of youth

And your mother's blood,

Both beseeching you to restore

A little faith in them!

Jerusalem

Jerusalem, O darlin',

I dream of you.

From the day I stepped on the heated rocks of the Nile,

You were there

With presentiments cuffed to my ankles.

A thousand fireflies billowed in my belly,

All shimmering,

All destined

To fly far and wide

Into the grimmest days of humankind.

There's not much of a *wrong* in wrongdoings

In a well of judgments.

There's *wrong* and there's *doings*.

Neither is mine to judge.

So I beseech you,

O Jerusalem,

To wait for me

Until I kiss myself goodnight!

Weaving a Republic!

So we sit and weave in circles,

An emblem of majestic pride and liberty,

Threads dipped in the cold bloody sweat

Of the Galwan Valley,

Grimacing at the faux hopes of farmers.

So we sit and weave in circles,

A symphony that was once a golden bird

Recalling forgotten folklore of the Deccan.

Did you forget the Sepoy Mutiny of 1857?

Or the dark, grim trenches of Jallianwala Bagh?

How they all came down with swords and rifles,

So we can sit and weave in circles?

Reading aloud a plethora of literature on civil discourse,

Those hard-sworn testimonies of Ambedkar

About our incessant dalliance with invasions,

Injustice, self-empowerment, and racism,

So today we proudly sit and weave in circles

In this golden cascade of a republic!

Urvashi Bundel

In Memory of Memorial Day

There's the America I've seen.

There's the America you've felt.

I've seen the America that celebrates sports like a ritual—

Yes, the Super Bowl.

I've seen the America that sings

In rambunctious bars at Madison Square Garden,

Rallying for human rights

Just because "we can,"

Dressed in ghastly Halloween attire,

Hustling in metros and the Port Authority terminal

With its "giant ratatouille,"

Queuing in rowdy lines for chipotle and hummus wraps

At Starbucks, an enterprise that's a crop of its own,

Growing like mushrooms in every nook and corner

Of New York City,

Where love is coffee and coffee is love,

Where the view of the Hudson River at sunset

Mesmerizes every passerby on Brooklyn Bridge.

I've seen the America that chased me down
In a Cabriolet, catcalling:
Hey, you! Babe! Listen, I love your heels!
The one that assembles in gratitude
And pain in Black churches,
Where choir is soul and soul is symphony.
And the one cradled in the decadence of Michigan Avenue,
Where Mother Teresa's words deck holy chambers.
I've seen America flock around its colossal centerpieces
With its ancient dinner sets
And new dreams on Thanksgiving,
Ruminating over past and present glories.
America that archives its history at the National Mall,
Flanked by the Smithsonian museums,
History that drifts down the Tidal Basin
Like cherry blossoms.
I've seen the America that rejoices and toasts to:
Give me your tired, your poor, your huddled masses
Yearning to breathe free.
America that fondly attributes
Manhattan's 102-story skyscraper to art.

America that takes pride in its civil rights movement
And the dissidence of the unruly.
America that celebrates its war heroes
With dignity and candor,
Solemnly saluting its stars and stripes.
America that is so colored and vigorously rainbowed,
Instilling hope in every migrant worker who touches its soil.
I've seen the America that embraces hardships
And stands tall no matter what.
America where strangers at a traffic signal stop
To applaud and say:
Congratulations on your graduation!
America that dines with its interracial magnitude
At think tanks on Massachusetts Avenue,
Embracing gender and sexual diversity.
I haven't forgotten the America
That believed in the power of its dreams
And in anyone who thought they had one.
But if today this is not true, just know
There's the America you've felt.
There's the America I've seen.

Waiting for the Sun to Rise

In your imperfect gorgeous antiquities,
I surrender my dusted hesitancy to frolic
Because gone are the days when we wondered
What anyone thought about our existence
And how we choose to exist.
Gone are the days when days were smarter
And nights ferociously sank their teeth
Into the crevices of digital mountains.
With you, time has become an illusion
Where minutes seem to age deeper than wine
Down in the casks of a forgotten cellar
Of time and space.
Isn't this what Einstein said about time?
The warm rays that often exude out of you
Make me want to say:
It has been so long.
I hope you've been doing well.

Duotones and Undertones

And there's so much that can be said

About love and friendships,

About life and death,

About time and the loss of it,

And our poignant ignorance towards them all.

And there's so much futility in reminiscing about them

Until you meet a soul so tender and kind,

Who makes you wonder about the multitones,

Duotones, and undertones—

Duotones of where you should be

And not where you are

And not where you want to be.

But all these murmurings are futile,

If you've not taken a leap of faith

In love and friendships.

And just like this prose,

It's such a simple thought

Which begins with an "and,"

Yet is hard to reconcile!

On Good and Bad Days

No matter how deep the unrest

Or roiling the turmoil,

You will rise

Till the time you believe

In the magic

Of rising.

So let's not rely on days anymore,

Or hope tomorrow will be a better day.

Let's rely on moments,

Good or bad.

Neither will last

Forever.

That's the magic you must hold onto!

Urvashi Bundel

Elderflower Women

Satisfied

To taste the glistening petals,

Like sheer white sheets

Covered with dewy essence,

Marmalade

With quintessential spreads

On crispy toast.

Dialed up with turbulent

Debates on the state of affairs

In states of affairs.

Dialed down with intellectuals

Competing to rein in minds

And feed opportunistic feats

Into deviant circles

Like overdosed tonics

Of questions!

Into meltdowns

Overpowered,

Underjudged,

Just how they like their coffee

And cocktails at glam-n-shams,

Filled with

Liquids crystalline as a glacier,

Sparkling with dizzy

Hints of sugar and florals

Enraptured.

Bad for sins.

Good for sinuses.

Brimming with unsigned contracts

Between tickling minds

And deserving hearts

At a twisted soirée

Filled with

Elderflower women!

Karnak Café: A Tribute

Inspired by a visit to the Egyptian cafe dedicated to Naguib Mahfouz, winner of the 1988 Nobel Prize for Literature.

At the midnight sun,

Between hours

Of insignificant chaos,

Of misunderstood echoes,

Of clandestine affairs,

There was a café

Where plots hatched.

It was called Karnak!

Bustling with intrigues

And unplayed games,

Bustling with shisha fumes

And unheard-of fames,

Karnak captured

The innocence of an author

Writing the romantic escapades

Of his early days.

Each corner divided,

Each corner dedicated,

Each corner bursting into flames

Of thrillers never heard,

Of illegal trade in lions and hawks,

Of disputed-land-grabbers,

Of petrified women hiding under veils,

Of content women called whores,

Of rebuked women driving the economy,

Of punished women writing books.

Karnak burned bright at night,

As it inhaled frozen thoughts

During the day.

It was Karnak, where men

Would sit and stare a whole day

And a whole night

Without interruption.

A busy new street, dazzling with

Old vintage cars,

Damsels in their twenties and thirties,

Rich with faux snake-leather shoes,

Walking down the street palely.

They smoked puffs of air

And sometimes

Air smoked them.

Karnak remained the vantage point

For both newbies and old,

For anyone desperately hawking

Old cars

And new women

In the desert!

Wild Openings!

Desperate times cry for desperate actions,

Actions that are quelled in the dungeons of our morality.

The days swing low and the nights taste like gold,

Shining so bright—

Shining through the unknown cavities

Of life and faith,

Filled with all its losses,

Wrapped around in the origami of inaction,

And letting it eat your cake.

Why not dissect it yourself, dear O dear?

Why do you wonder so hard?

Miseries shall come and go.

Hold your head up high, gentlemen.

The door is open.

The door is open wide.

The strangest things happen when least expected

Through the light and shadows.

So take that leap of faith

And fly!

July's Buck Moon

Lilies, I've seen them

Used—a dysfunctional use

That sometimes makes me wonder

If they merely bloom to fill the gaps among the dead.

Mostly the mortal ones,

The sophistication with which they blossom.

Is that what the full Buck Moon often aspires to?

In the middle of the night and otherwise,

When the lightning strikes in Capricornus,

The hermit loses his vestigial search.

And in the hours of heavy deluge,

Between obedience and revolt,

Eclipses last a lifetime

Like holy matrimonies

Signed between astronomy and astrology

Of the unfashionable type,

In search of a breathing star.

We, too, could rise like the Thunder Moon,

Rising from the occluded postulates

Of our penumbral shadows.

We, too, could overcome our dissidence

In the wake of wisdom,

Searching

Like the Three Wise Men

Who chose never to give up!

A Better Day

My lavender dreams frolic

Like Spanish wild horses

Chasing the wind,

For tomorrow will be a better day.

That I can't promise,

But I promise

That I'll be here

To hear you say

What a day it is!

A Woman's Prerogative

Even flowers bloom

From broken pots,

From ruined crevices of abandoned walls,

From desolate rocks on the riverside.

And you,

You are but a human being!

Sparrow

Clipped

Tears,

Fears,

Chiseled jaws,

Chiseled heart,

Dark eyes,

Dark wings

In darker alleys.

She's unstoppable—

Immolates

Like a legendary phoenix,

Rising from her ashes—

Not a sparrow.

See what I have?

The cage screeches.

Now I know why Maya Angelou's

Caged bird

Sings!

Urvashi Bundel

On Never Giving Up!

I see you go

Into the mist,

Into far-stretched lands.

I see you fade

Into the land of sun.

But now, I marvel:

Who's braver?

You,

The sunflower,

Or the one

That turns!

The Art of Climbing

I made peace with you a long time ago,
In the epicurean center of your dilapidated heart,
Swinging between the low of things and the high of life.
I urge you to see beyond the contemporary noise
That's sweeping our tabletops and deserting our wineries
With a shrill sound that overflows
In the basement of your frail, docile heart.
I urge you to curb those nerves ensconced in this moment,
See beyond the caves of your past.
I want you to see past the wide valleys of your present—
Those pinnacles of snowy hardships
And rocky cliffs which you feared to climb—
To reach a point where all you can see is the future.
Isn't it beautiful?
I told you the view is always beautiful from the top!

About the Author

Born in India, Urvashi Bundel has lived and worked across America, Africa, Asia, Australia, and Europe as an international law practitioner and defender of refugee rights with the United Nations Refugee Agency and other international firms, like Deloitte. She is the first Indian recipient of the Monbukagakusho (MEXT) Honors Scholarship from the Global Business Leaders Program run by the Japanese government. Urvashi was awarded a National Book Fair Award in India for poetry in 2004. She holds degrees from Johns Hopkins University SAIS (Italy/USA) and Ritsumeikan APU (Japan); and she has received academic recognitions from Leiden University (the Netherlands) and the Peter McMullin Centre on Statelessness, Melbourne Law School (Australia). In *Unapologetically Feminist*, Urvashi uses her energetic language to tackle the complex subjects of patriotism, immigration, and human rights.